Farm
Alphabet Book

Farm Alphabet Book

Jane Miller

J.M. Dent & Sons Ltd

London   Melbourne

First published 1981
Reprinted 1982, 1984
© Jane Miller 1981
Designed by Malcolm Young
Phototypeset in Great Britain by
Filmtype Services Limited, Scarborough
Printed and bound in Singapore
by Tien Wah PTE Ltd
for J.M. Dent & Sons Ltd
Aldine House, Welbeck Street, London
ISBN 0 460 06979 9

The author would like to thank the following for their
invaluable help and assistance with this book:
June Armstrong
Richard Baker and Andrew Budd, Preshaw Estate, Hampshire
Patricia Blake
Keira Glen
Sue Latham
Poultry World
Norman Simmons
Yeo Bros. (A. N. Yeo) Ltd., Bristol

To Jean Brooker who started the whole idea

A a

apple

Apples are
picked in
the late
summer and
autumn,
when they
are ripe.

D d

donkey

Donkeys graze in the fields when they are not pulling carts.

E e

egg

Birds lay
eggs.
These eggs
were laid
by a hen.

Ff

foal

A foal is a young horse.
Its mother is a mare.
Its father is a stallion.

G g

goat

A young goat
is a kid.
Its mother is
a nanny-goat.
Its father is
a billy-goat.

H h

hen

A hen is the
mother of
a chick.
The chick's
father is
a cockerel.

I i

incubator

An incubator
keeps eggs
warm.
After 21 days
chicks
hatch out
of the eggs.

Jj

jam

Jam is made from fruit boiled with sugar and water.

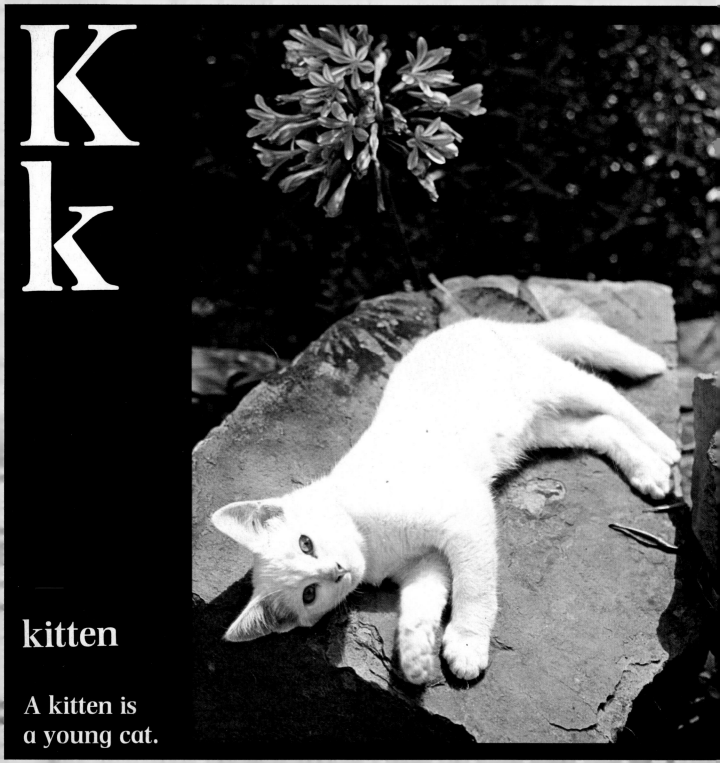

K k

kitten

A kitten is
a young cat.

Ll

lamb

A lamb is a young sheep.
Its mother is a ewe.
Its father is a ram.

Mm

mouse

A mouse sleeps during the day and finds its food at night.

N
n

nest

Nests are built by birds to lay their eggs in. This is a coot's nest.

O o

orchard

**Fruit trees
grow in
orchards.**

Pp

pig

This is a mother pig, called a sow.
A father pig is a boar.
A young pig is a piglet.

Q
q

quill

A quill is a
large feather.
It grows in
a bird's wing
or tail.
A quill can be
used as a pen.

Rr

rabbit

Tame rabbits are kept as pets. Wild rabbits live in burrows under the ground.

S s

swan

A mother
swan teaches
her cygnets
to swim
as soon
as they are
hatched.

Tt

tractor

Tractors pull machines on the farm.

Uu

umbrella

Umbrellas keep people dry when it rains.

V v

vegetable

Vegetables
are grown
on farms and
in gardens.

W
W

web

Webs are
spun by
spiders.
In these they
catch insects
to eat.

X

X shows that this sheep
and lamb
belong to the farmer.

Y y

yolk

A yolk is the yellow p[c]
of an egg.

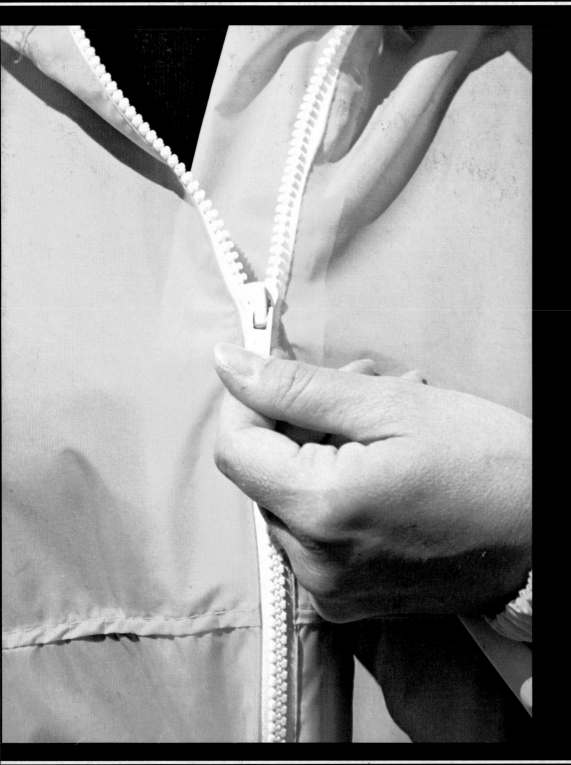

Z z

zip

Zips open and close all kinds of clothes worn on the farm.

Jane Miller was born and brought up in Australia.
At the age of ten she was taking photographs of the animals
she owned, and processing them herself using a printing frame
and printing-out paper. Before coming to London in 1958,
Jane Miller visited Thailand and India where she took many
photographs that have since been published. She subsequently
trained as a free-lance photographer and began to work
professionally, travelling widely in the British Isles.
Her photographs now appear in magazines, newspapers and
books, as well as on calendars and greetings cards.
Jane Miller's other highly successful photographic books,
published by **Dent**, are *Birth of a Foal, Lambing Time, A Calf is
Born, Farm Counting Book* **and** *Birth of Piglets.*